Dat~so~la~lee
Artisan

Written by Gayle Ross

Illustrated by Sam Sam Burrus

MODERN CURRICULUM PRESS

Program Reviewers

Cathy White Eagle, Executive Director
and President of the Board
Eagle Vision Educational Network
Granite Bay, California

Jeffrey Hamley, Director
Native American Program
Harvard University
Cambridge, Massachusetts

Gwen Sebastian Hill, Teacher
Development Trainer
District of Philadelphia
Philadelphia, Pennsylvania

Paulette Molin, Ph. D., Assistant Dean
The Graduate College
Hampton University
Hampton, Virginia

Joan Webkamigad, Education Specialist
Michigan Department of Education
Lansing, Michigan

Executive Editor: Janet Rosenthal
Project Editors: Elizabeth Wojnar
                       Mark Shelley

MODERN CURRICULUM PRESS

An imprint of Paramount Supplemental Education
250 James Street
Morristown, New Jersey 07960

ISBN 0-8136-5734-2   (Reinforced Binding)   0-8136-5740-7   (Paperback)
Library of Congress Catalog Card Number: 94-077306

10 9 8 7 6 5 4 3 2 1   SP   99 98 97 96 95 94

Dear Reader,

What are some of your favorite things to do? Dat-so-la-lee loved to weave baskets. They reminded her of her life as a member of the Washo Nation.

Dat-so-la-lee did not have an easy life. She worked hard and faced many problems with courage.

Read about Dat-so-la-lee and why she was so famous for weaving baskets. As you read, think about what you would like to do if you had the chance.

Your friend,

Gayle Ross

To the people of the Washo Nation, the
birth of a baby was a time of great joy.
A new baby was welcomed with
prayers and songs. When Dat-so-la-lee
was born in 1835, her parents called
her Dabuda. She was wrapped in a
rabbit-skin blanket and placed in a
special oval-shaped basket.

1

When Dabuda was about one month old, a feast was held for her. Her mother and father served a large meal. They also gave gifts to their family and friends. Dabuda's parents did this to show how happy they were to have a new baby.

3

4

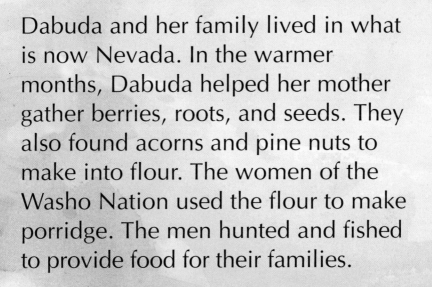

Dabuda and her family lived in what is now Nevada. In the warmer months, Dabuda helped her mother gather berries, roots, and seeds. They also found acorns and pine nuts to make into flour. The women of the Washo Nation used the flour to make porridge. The men hunted and fished to provide food for their families.

In the winter months, Dabuda's father made arrow tips. Dabuda and her mother wove baskets and made clothing for the family.

The women of the Washo Nation made many different kinds of baskets. There were baskets for gathering pine cones and for holding food. Some tightly woven baskets could even hold water!

Dabuda quickly learned how to make baskets. She split stalks from branches of the willow tree and formed them into a circle. Dabuda then sewed the coils together with thread. The thread was made from the inner bark of willow stalks.

Dabuda's mother and other women taught her how to make designs on the baskets. Dabuda learned so quickly and wove so well that people said, "Dabuda has magic in her fingers."

When Dabuda was about ten years old, life for the Washo began to change. Gold was found in California, and many people traveled through Washo land to get there.

In 1859, gold and silver were found on Washo land. Many settlers rushed to this area. The settlers changed the land by cutting down trees and building towns. The Washo tried to keep their way of life alive, but things were changing very quickly.

11

Dabuda's life was changing, too. She married a Washo man named Assu. Because they needed money to live, Assu and Dabuda had to work on a ranch in Carson Valley, Nevada.

This was not a happy time for Dabuda. She and her husband had two children. At a young age, both of their children got sick and died. Then Assu died, too. He froze to death while trying to cross the Sierra Nevada Mountains in the winter.

Dabuda was sad after her children and husband died. She moved to the mining town of Monitor, California. There she worked for a family named Cohn. Dabuda took care of their young son, Abe. She no longer had time to weave her beautiful baskets.

After a few years, Dabuda married Charley Keyser, who was also a Washo. Since the Washo people did not have last names, Charley took his last name from the owners of the ranch where he worked. Then Dabuda changed her name to Louisa Keyser.

Louisa and Charley were happy together. Charley was known for the beautiful flint arrow tips he made. Louisa started weaving baskets again. This helped keep the memory of her Washo childhood alive.

In 1895, Louisa brought four glass bottles covered with woven willow into a store in Carson City, Nevada. Abe Cohn, the little boy she had once cared for, now owned the store.

Abe liked the bottles, but he told Louisa that people really loved baskets. He asked Louisa, "Could you weave some baskets for me to sell?" Louisa said, "Yes!"

21

Louisa's baskets sold as fast as Abe could put them out in his store. Abe wanted more baskets than Louisa had time to make. Finally he and Louisa made a deal. Abe would pay all of Louisa's and Charley's living costs. In return, Louisa would spend all of her time weaving baskets for Abe to sell.

Soon, people from across the United States heard of Louisa and her baskets. She was called "Queen of the Washo Basketmakers." About this time, she changed her name to Dat-so-la-lee. She may have done this to honor a friend.

Dat-so-la-lee continued to weave baskets until she was over eighty years old. Before she died on December 6, 1925, she had made over 300 baskets for Abe. Today Dat-so-la-lee's baskets are found in museums across the United States.

Glossary

artisan (är′tə zən) someone who makes things that need a special skill

feast (fēst) a very large meal with many different courses

flint (flint) a hard stone that is used to make arrowheads. It can also be used to start a fire.

porridge (pôr′ij) a kind of soup made from grains or nuts that is boiled with water until it is thick. Oatmeal is a kind of porridge.

settler (set′lər) a person who moves to a new place to live

About the Author

Gayle Ross is a direct descendant of John Ross, Principal Chief of the Cherokee Nation during the time of the Trail of Tears. Since 1979, Ms. Ross has traveled the United States telling Native American stories at schools, libraries, colleges, and festivals. She has recorded two audio tapes of Cherokee stories, and her Cherokee Rabbit stories have been collected in a book. The author lives with her husband, Reed Holt, and two children, Alan and Sarah, in Fredericksburg, Texas.

About the Illustrator

Sam Sam Burrus is a resident of Albuquerque, New Mexico. She was born into the Paint Clan of the Cherokee Nation of Oklahoma. From the time she was a girl, drawing and painting have helped Ms. Burrus to share with others her stories and joy of living. In *Dat-so-la-lee,* she used watercolor and crayon to celebrate Dat-so-la-lee's life.